BRYCE THOMPSON

MILLIONS

ACCEPTED & EXCEPTED

EXPERIENCES AND LESSONS

Paperback: ISBN 978-1-7341227-4-9
Ebook ISBN 978-1-7341227-5-6

Library of Congress Cataloging-in-Publication Data
https://lccn.loc.gov/2021913473
Thompson, Bryce. Millions accepted and excepted: experiences and lessons / Bryce Thompson. Los Angeles, CA: B. Thompson Management Corp, 2021.
pages cm 121.
ISBN: 978-1-7341227-4-9

Book / Cover designs by Bryce Thompson
Author Photos by Sean Coleman

Printed in the United States of America

Contents

Introduction

I've learned "to whom much is given, much shall be required" is both Biblical fruition and continuum. Life is life no matter who you are or what you have. The tests are for the testimony, the trails are for the travel, trials to become triumphs, perseverance for purpose and the gifts are for the gratitude and the giving.

Honestly, as much as I am happy about all of this, there is an uneasiness that comes with it. Since I've become successful, this feeling is more of a norm than I could have ever imagined. So, for this reason, I've come to understand the meaning of and the importance of being gracious and the happiness in that. With more success, more money, and more recognition there will be things and problems that arise that most people probably would never think they would have to deal with. The successful version of you lives in a different life than you right now. And even with all the success, yes, most of it will be accepted, but you will still face trials of it being excepted as well.

As much as people want to know me, there is so much more to know than just me. Life lessons are the best lessons. It's even better when we share our experiences allowing us to learn from each other. While the dreams and desire to succeed served as motivation, what I've learned made me who I am, and now it all does make sense.

Your goals are your goals and no one else's. Why would you expect for anybody to work for and believe in them the way that you do?
... they're yours

Chapter 1
FORBES

I knew eventually I would end up in LA, but since I moved here, there have been times when the COVID-19 shutdowns and restrictions made me feel like I may have moved a little too soon. Today, I was reminded why I don't believe in luck, or second guess my gut feelings. When I see opportunities to get closer to my goals, I capitalize on them. Having this mindset has paid off many times before, and driving my Wraith down Santa Monica Boulevard, taking in the Cali vibes and scenery, I realized it paid off again.

It had been a pretty chill morning. I had spent it working out and visiting two of my closest friends. I was heading home when the text notification chimed on my phone. While I know I shouldn't have, I did anyway. I took my eyes off the road to check the text, which turned out to be a link from Forbes.com with my face and name attached to it. It still seemed unbelievable. Without hesitation, I went ahead and clicked the link. "Damn," right there, there it was. I was in Forbes.

Seeing my picture underneath the Forbes title was big for me. Forbes wasn't always my dream or the biggest goal I had growing up, but seeing my name under the Forbes title was still significant. I could only think back to how far I've come and how this was bigger than just me because seeing this happen for me could inspire people like me, people in my industry, millennials, and young Black men and women to realize that even with all odds against them, they can do it too.

I honestly can't recall the exact feeling at the time this happened, but I would say the moment was definitely special. I got to meet with a Forbes writer a few weeks before it happened. I was a little concerned of what the article would say because I had no input on how it would be written, but it was everything I wanted it to be and more. The names of all the people who have been significant to my business, the people who have been on this ride with me, were there along with mine. All my big accomplishments over the past four years were highlighted. My latest goal, starting an HBCU scholarship, was the focus of the write-up. It was a blessing to know that wanting to pay it forward by giving to others had helped me reach a goal of being featured in Forbes. I never personally knew anyone in Forbes, so I guess I made it more common and attainable for the people who know me. From dream to vision, to goal to physical. "Meet Bryce Thompson: 24 Year Old..." was the headline in Forbes.

I shared the link with friends and family as I continued the drive home, but the voice I wanted to hear the most was my Mom's. It's funny because my college senior year, I was nominated "Most Likely to be Featured in Forbes," which at the time was crazy. But shortly after that happened, I had shared with my Mom that as far-fetched as it may have seemed, I really wanted it to happen, and I believed it would. Always my biggest supporter, she believed, too. Now here we were on the phone talking about the actual feature right in front of me. Through her tears and telling me how proud of me she was, she reminded me of our conversation three years ago, "This is what you wanted Bryce…" It was more than what I had wanted, it was what I had seen in my dreams, and I made manifesting my dream my goal.

So today, my emotions nor the feature were new. It was like my birthday; I knew at its time it would come. I just didn't think it would happen the way it happened as fast as it had happened, but when it's your time, it's your time. I'm blessed. It was my time.

Once I made it home, I took the time to post and share the link with friends and family, which sent my phone into a frenzy. While I responded to the nonstop congratulatory phone calls and texts, I realized more and more how powerful it was and how real the accomplishment had become. As I said before, being featured in Forbes had always been a goal. Now that this had happened in real life, I had to take a moment to think about and reflect on how all this was manifested. It took a little minute to hit me, but eventually it did.

Literally within like thirty days from the initial meeting I had with the Forbes writer, it was reality. I had recently acquired a new business manager and mentioned to her one of my goals was to have an article in Forbes. I had met with the writer previously but didn't know he was a contributor for Forbes. As it always is when the stars align, my business manager knew him as well. After sharing my goal to be in Forbes, a meeting had been arranged between the writer and I in which we briefly discussed him doing a feature on me for Forbes. I was grateful for the meeting, but this wasn't the first time someone had told me they would help me achieve my goal of being featured. In all honesty, I wasn't pressed or holding my breath. After we met, three weeks or so went by before I heard from him again. However, he kept his word and did exactly what he said he would do. My interview didn't happen the way I had imagined, but after meeting with him, I was pretty confident that he would write up a story on me. The next time I heard from the writer again, it was him sending me the link to the feature.

Being featured in Forbes had become more than just a goal for me or for my own self-fulfillment. I wanted to pay homage to my friends and those significant to the whole journey. It was even more fulfilling to have the article be centered around me paying it forward and helping HBCU students go to school.

BT Lesson

SETTING & MANIFESTING GOALS

The lesson I want to share here is the power of setting goals. It's important to set both short-term and long-term goals. However, the long-term goals are the ones most manifested, while the short-term goals are goals that you can start and execute immediately. Most times people get so caught up on the long-term objective, that they forget about what they can do in the present that will point them and lead them to where they want to be in the future, long-term.

You can't get so caught up on the top of the mountain that you trip over the rock that's right in front of you.
While Forbes was a long-term goal that I manifested, working hard, fine-tuning, and paying very close attention to details as far as my business was concerned is what got me there.

You may have a goal of being a millionaire, but don't forget you still have to first make six figures. Before you can make six figures, you first have to make five figures. Better yet, in all things, fitness, education, financial, etc., you can be one step better today than you were yesterday, and every step you take right now is necessary for where you want to be when it's all said and done.

Your short-term goals are in the conscious mind, while your long-term goals are in the subconscious mind. What you actively do in the present, your day-to-day activities, is the result of your conscious mind. Even if you do it unconsciously in the form of a habit. For example, you brush your teeth daily out of habit, to maintain hygiene and fresh breath. That's the short-term, conscious, focused goal. This daily consistent habit, this routine, along with routine dental visits, support the subconscious, long-term goal of preventing cavities, preserving your teeth, and overall good health.

It's important to know that what you actively do in the physical, present day-to-day is pulled from your conscious mind. But it is just as important to know and remember that what you see and what and who you surround yourself with in your conscious, daily, present day-to-day will be stored in your subconscious mind and impact the long-term goals that you set. Your daily habits and the people and environments you surround yourself with should consciously support your long-term goals. Adjust habits and surroundings as necessary regularly.

Stare where you want to be in the face every day. My house was once my wallpaper, and my car was once my screensaver. I went into stores I wanted to shop at and tried on clothes and jewelry I couldn't afford before I could afford them. All my goals were written on my bathroom mirror before I ever accomplished them.

forgetting where
you come from
will leave you
feeling lost.

Chapter 2
THE SLAB STILL STANDS

Home is where the heart is. Even though my heart no longer resides here, my foundation is rooted here. I came here today with the intention to simply capture video footage; footage that may never be more than an archived record, but regardless of the purpose, I know it needs to be captured. Now standing in the driveway I realize how much this home is a big part of me. Growing up here in this home, in Missouri City, Texas, is significant to who I am.

It seems like it has been a while since I last went inside, and as I'm staring towards the door, I feel the urge to walk up and knock, but I don't. The place that I had known for most of my life as the home I could always return to is no longer mine to enter. My Mom sold this house about two years ago, and now standing here I would buy it today if I could, but it's not for sale.

I am blessed to say most of my childhood memories here were good ones. I still remember when we first moved in, and the excitement I felt about living in a home for the first time. Before this, most of my childhood was spent moving from apartment complex to apartment complex. I remember the first time I saw it, I literally thought to myself, *Wow, this is lit.* My Mom let me paint my room blue, which was my favorite color at the time. Wow, it's crazy, so many things I thought I had forgotten start to come back to me, as I wonder if my old room is still blue now. "Probably not." The house was huge to me back then, and even though it could fit into the places I live now, it's still a big part of my life. Never get too big for the small things.

It seems as if it was just yesterday that I was a kid walking underneath the bayou that's just around the corner from the house. Standing here, I allow myself to do something I rarely get to do these days. I embrace the moment and let my mind take me back to simpler times as a kid when nothing mattered but video games, playing basketball, and meeting girls at school. I look to my right at the corner where I would run to catch the bus for school. I hear myself laugh before I can stop it over the fact that I can't stop myself from smiling like the kid I was back then as I think about how my Mom helped me pick out clothes for school.

My memories are not the typical traditional memories of family dinners and holidays. Even though I always liked Christmas, we didn't really celebrate Christmas, which I think was mainly because it wasn't recognized by the church we attended at that time. At least that's what my Mom told us, but now that I know what I know, it was an extra expense for the year that she knew she couldn't add on. Needless to say, I celebrate Christmas now. Funny, I just bought my first Christmas tree this year, and not a cheap one either.

We moved a couple of times, but we always came back here. This was home. The first time we moved was because we were robbed one time. That is probably the worst thing that ever happened here. Someone literally broke into our home and stole what, at the time, was my most prized possession and the one thing I was not willing to lose, all my X-box games. They actually didn't steal the X-box, just all my X-box games. I still don't understand why they didn't take the X-box. They just took the games. It's a good thing we weren't home when it happened.

As a kid, I really had a lot of fun. Now I'm thinking to myself and laughing, looking at the spot in the yard where my older brother used to have me box, like a member of a fight club. Not a literal fight club, but he would have me put on the gloves and box other little kids in the neighborhood. Still laughing and shaking my head at the fact that I used to literally put on gloves and box and put on a show for the street we lived on. If we knew then what we know now, we definitely would have charged a viewing fee. But now that I am thinking about it, me boxing back then is not too far off because I always had a "why not" mentality; you'll never know until you make an attempt. Which reminds me, I remember knocking myself out cold and breaking my wrist in this same house because I slid down the staircase banister copying Sonic the Hedgehog ®. Thank God my Mom found me, because when I regained conscious, I was at the hospital with a broken wrist and a busted lip.

The basketball goal that was midway in the driveway where my brother and I used to play one-on-one is no longer here. This is one of the main places where my obsession with basketball developed. We would play late into the night. The more I played, the better I got but it's time to go. These days it seems it's always time to go. I have enjoyed this short moment of memories.

Stepping back into the SUV, I notice the foundation that once supported the brick mailbox, and I stop. The brick mailbox had been knocked down years ago by one of our drunk neighbors. It's funny that a brand new mailbox has been built right beside it, but the foundation of the original mailbox, maybe five inches high of brick and concrete, still remains there in the grass. To any person it may seem tacky for the foundation and new mailbox to stand side by side, but I think it's really cool that I not only remember how it happened but also find meaning in why it's still there.

BT Lesson

EVERYTHING NEEDS FOUNDATION

The most important part of anything, organization business, family, or any great creation, is the foundation it is built on. You identify the end from the beginning. You must know what you want to build before you can start building. You identify the desired outcome at the start of the process. Before you lay one brick or hammer one nail, you must develop the foundation, and the foundation must be strong enough to support every outcome.

Success is dreams realized, and dreams are realized through the accomplishment of a series of goals. Achieving goals to realize dreams is just like building a house. The rooms within the house are the goals that, combined, equate to the overall dream. The foundation is the place where goals are placed upon for the overall dream to stand on. The final house is the dream, the success. When the house becomes a home, the dream is realized. This is why the beginning is just as important as the end, and the end is just as important as the beginning. The outcome is just as important as the start, and the start is just as important as the outcome.

You can build a house of wood very fast, but if the right storm comes, it will be gone just as fast. You can build a house of brick, and it may take a lot longer to knock it down, but storms demolish brick houses, too. No matter what storm comes around to tear a house down, a solid foundation will still be there long after the storm has come, and the house is gone.

Too many people get caught up and discouraged over not getting somewhere fast or in a certain desired, or their planned, timeframe. The reality is there is value in enjoying and being glad that you haven't reached the desired outcome, because this is a signal that there is more time to focus on building and solidifying what will be there forever, the foundation. The only thing worse than not getting something or getting somewhere is getting a taste of it and losing it. The losses are usually because the goal is unsustainable, because the foundation can't hold it. If the foundation cannot support the goal, a room per say, it surely isn't strong enough to support the dream, the entire house. A house may remain on an unstable foundation, but it will be beat up with a lot of problems. Don't ever be upset about still being in the beginning, building the foundation, because once that's solid, you can always keep building and rebuilding. The fortunate part is the more time you spend there, the stronger it'll be to continue to build upon and fall back on later. So be grateful in the foundation phase and embrace and appreciate the growth.

Don't put so much focus on the efficiency that you lose sight of the effectiveness. No matter how far you get, it should still bring you back to where you discovered the overall goal in the first place, which is the foundation. You should never be impressed with what you've become or where you've gotten until you can lose what you've gotten and rebuild it back. It's more than just building it, it's more than just making it. That's the easy part. Keeping it is hard; maintaining it is even harder. It is disappointing not having it, but it is even more painful to get it and lose it. This is why I urge people to avoid getting caught up and focused on what you don't have. God and the Universe are doing you a favor. If you don't have it, it's because you're not ready for it. So it's a blessing for you to not have it yet. Be grateful for the process because it's going to help you appreciate and value it more when you do actually have what you want. Certain people are in certain places for a reason. Don't waste time or give energy to wondering why them and not you. It's not always because they're better or smarter. It's more so because they probably can just handle it better at that specific time, or worse, they could have taken shortcuts to get it and are on the brink of losing it. Don't get "it" not being your time confused with "it" not being your purpose. What you want is for you, it is your purpose. Stay committed and do the work, do it the right way, take the necessary time so it will be worth it and not in vain. Don't get to day ninety-nine to slow down, quit, and give up, because day one hundred could be the day that will change everything. It may just not be your time. Put in the work, and more importantly, put in the time; however, long it takes. It'll be worth it. You can always rebuild if you start with a solid foundation.

Even though the mailbox is gone and has been gone for over ten years, the foundation remains, and it could still hold a new brick mailbox if it needed to. More than that, no matter how many mailboxes are built up around it, it still holds its place. It is still a foundation where at any time a new mailbox can be built, on that same slab of solid brick.

I laughed about fighting in the yard, but now it all makes sense. Standing here now, I feel more in tune with who I am. I can see how people can forget where they come from and end up feeling lost. Just like the foundation of the brick mailbox still stands even though the mailbox is long gone, the determination, focus, and fight in me that developed in this yard boxing and hooping still stands. This tenacity to persevere through and never quit serves me well to this day because this success isn't easy at all. It's more fighting and pushing through than flossing, celebratory bottle popping, and parties.

I identified my desired outcome early in my life, at the start of my foundational process. To put it metaphorically, I didn't know what the house looked like exactly or how many rooms it had, but I knew I wanted a mansion. I knew I wanted to achieve massive success, so along with the values instilled by my parents, I started adding the right ingredients to ensure I had a foundation that could support the success I envisioned for myself. The first thing I added was doing well in school, because education and knowledge are something I could always build on. Still to this day, the more I learn, the better I become in all aspects of life.

Embrace the bottom the same way you think you would embrace the top if you were there already. When you reach the sky, don't lose touch with what it was like on the ground.

I just decided to give something a large portion of me.

Chapter 3
FOCUSED
OBSESSION

I don't remember the exact moment, day, or year, but I was in my elementary school when I decided my route to a successful life was the NBA. I had many examples of professional athletes that aligned with my vision of success. Professional sports guaranteed monetary wealth and the lifestyle I envisioned for myself. Even that early, I understood college was a stepping-stone into the NBA, so getting into a good school was a necessity that I had already started working towards. Once I made the decision that basketball was my ticket, I stayed committed to being an athlete and doing well in school.

When I have an idea or want to do something, I don't like to waste time. I just do it, because the ninety-nine percent of the people who aren't successful actually have ideas more genius than the one percent of people who are. I am competitive, not to the point of competing to dominate others, but to be better than I was before and to inspire other people. Being an inspiration is a good feeling, but more than that, I want others to see I had the courage and be inspired.

I dedicated myself to developing myself as a basketball player, or in other words, a hooper. I studied the game as much as I practiced. When I was not in my books, I was on the basketball courts perfecting my craft. I became focused to the point of obsession. During the school day, I focused on my books, and once I was out of class, I ate, slept, and drank basketball. I would play basketball by myself or one-on-one with my older brother until it got dark and even into the night. Sometimes when it got dark, I would dribble in the garage for hours. Obsession paid off.

Basketball was my ticket to success, and it was also how I networked with people and made new friends.
Outside of school ball, I also played competitively over the summer. I had played for the best teams in the city and got invited to the most elite camps along with all the best players around the country by the time I was going into high school.

Once I reached my sophomore year of high school, I started getting more attention from colleges and receiving letters in the mail. None of the letters were from high level universities, and that was when I started to realize the possibility of the NBA not being my ticket to success. I wasn't discouraged, because at the same time, I would still be able to do what I love and play at the collegiate level, network and make new friends beyond high school.

I played for a public high school in the heart of Houston, Texas, my freshman year, but the basketball program was not the best, so I transferred to a different school my sophomore year just to be in a better basketball program. The year I transferred, the school had recruited and brought in three to five of the best players around the city. They were a little older than me, but I still shared the court with them. I played varsity my first year I transferred. This is when I started getting attention from colleges, and the top summer ball teams were reaching out to me to play with them over the summer.

The summer after my sophomore year in high school is when things started picking up for me in basketball. I was traveling all around the country playing on a bigger and bigger stage every time I played. I remember being in Vegas that year, and college coaches were literally asking me what time I was playing because they wanted to come to the game to actually watch me play. At this point, my confidence and the reality of me playing ball at the collegiate level was through the roof.

Me being in Vegas was one of the most memorable stages I had played on, but it was also one of the most pivotal. I was on the stage. The lights were on me, and I was performing at a high level. But at the same time, this is where my life took a detour. Post tournament I came back home to Houston and after a few days I started feeling a tingling going down my left leg. I didn't pay it any mind, but the tingling started going down to my feet. Then my toes would go numb on and off. The pain and uncomfortable feeling progressively got worse and carried on into my junior year of high school. Some days I would limp to class, and I would just pop a pain pill every day to just get rid of the pain.

I hated the doctors, so I never went. My Mom kept asking me if I was okay and if everything was fine, but I didn't want to worry her and I was in denial at the same time. It got to a point I wasn't able to sit at my desk in class, so my teachers started allowing me to lay on the floor. When that wasn't enough, I would excuse myself for hours to go to the nurse so I could lay down. It wasn't until I had to pop more than one pain pill a day to keep the pain from coming back that I started to consider seeing a doctor. The pain eventually became too bad to even walk, so I had to go to the doctor.

Once I went to the doctor, they did an MRI and multiple X-rays. I remember sitting in the waiting room nervous as I waited to find out what was really wrong with me. The doctor came and told me I had one herniated disk and a ruptured disk in the lower lumbar of my back. They gave me two options. I could have surgery and potentially have back problems later on as I got older, or I could just all around stop playing basketball. I didn't choose either one. So my entire junior year, I popped multiple pain pills every single day just to play through it. It affected the way I played, and I didn't feel like myself on the court. I just wasn't the same player. But, I was still good enough to help lead my team to a state championship that year and still get some college attention.

That summer going into my senior year, I decided not to play as competitively to give my back a break and prepare for my high school senior season. Unfortunately, life hit me. It hit me hard really for the first time in my life. I had damaged my back so bad that I couldn't even pass a physical to play. I physically was not able to turn my body certain ways or do certain stretches. I had almost crippled myself. And now I was forced to make the decision to not play basketball anymore. I had to spend almost six months in physical therapy just to be able to sit in my chair properly in school. Eventually my body healed back enough to get back my normal capabilities, but I still had to sit on the bench my entire senior year and watch from the sidelines in my warm-up suit.

I had to come to grips that I could no longer play at the collegiate level, either. I guess this is the point when I realized I had a different purpose.

BT Lesson

EXCUSES WON'T EXCUSE YOU

At the beginning of 2021, I wrote on my social media, "How you start is usually because of your parents, but where you end up is all on you. It's really no excuse for what happens when you leave home because from that point it's all on you." Now that I'm writing this book and sharing what I learned at these pivotal points in my life, I realize there's never really an excuse to just quit. Even when things happen that are beyond your control, even when you've dedicated yourself to making it happen. Even when you've developed a solid plan and executed every single step. There is never an excuse to just throw your hands up and quit. The tenacity you developed to accomplish that goal or that original plan is still there. It's the tenacity that you need to hold on to because plans will fail, plans will change, but that fight in you is what will see you through, and if you just pivot to focus on the next plan, that same tenacity can help you.

Now, there is a difference between being tenacious and just doing the most. Sometimes you have to realize and accept your plan is not the plan. I planned to make my living in the NBA, but that wasn't it for me. The dream to live the way I live, have a positive impact on young people like myself, give back to my community, and retire my parents was on point. It just wasn't meant for me to be able to do it with basketball. Basketball was there to help me develop my commitment, to help me develop my networking skills, and to help me realize my grit. It's important to know and remember there are twenty-six letters in the alphabet, so if plan A doesn't work, it doesn't mean that's not your purpose, it's usually the requirement to activate Plan B, Plan C, and so on until you reach where you ultimately want to go.

Everything I did from boxing in the yard, to getting good grades in school, to hooping, to getting into college was part of the plan, but it was also part of the purpose. It wasn't a total loss just because I wasn't going to play ball in college or the NBA.

My dedication and determination to play professional ball was the reason I not only practiced playing, I studied the game and mastered the fundamentals both physically and mentally. Well, guess what, I applied that same dedication and practiced trading and investing and studied to master the fundamentals in business the same way. My focus with school and basketball taught me to prioritize, avoid negative influences, and make the necessary trade-offs to be successful. That same focus is what I fell back on to start and build my business. There were times I could have been out partying or used the money I was investing in my business to pay bills or buy stuff, but instead I made the sacrifice then and it's still paying off now. I had learned as a kid to be responsible and hold myself accountable to my schoolwork as well as my teammates.

It's important to learn how to focus and stay focused on what you want and where you're trying to go. It's important to build a level of obsession that strengthens your grit, your tenacity for what you want to do at that time as well as in the future.

My ability to persevere has served me well. When something is difficult, I do it over and over again, until I perfect it. After I've perfected it, I still keep working on it because there is always room for improvement. To me, the comfort zone is the place where failure takes hold. Being balanced keeps you leveled, but when you're leveled, you can't level up. There's no climb in balance.

As I close this lesson, I want to emphasize the value of having the determination to stay true to yourself and true to the visions you have for yourself and your future. I never had to study that. I never had to study me. No matter how many letdowns I've faced or how many times I've had to take it back to the drawing board and pivot, the main goal of living a successful life and having a positive impact on people like myself has never changed. This is why I don't, and won't, quit. Quitting is never an option. This is not a new concept but rather a tried and true concept that I apply to everything I do. Don't let distractors, deterrents, stop you. Remind yourself regularly of what you've set out to accomplish, and no matter how many times you have to adjust the plan or challenges arise, never accept any excuse to miss out on achieving the things you've envisioned for you. I didn't make it to the NBA, but a few people that joined my business did.

It's crazy what can happen when you don't compete, you just huddle...

Chapter 4

DEAR OLD MOREHOUSE

I wish the people I meet now could have known me when I didn't have anything, when I didn't have a dollar in my bank account. I wish people had the opportunity to witness when I was at the point of only having a dream, and I couldn't even afford to go to sleep to dream again if I wanted to. The only way I could sleep, the only way I could be content with not getting to the next level, was knowing I had given all I had to achieving the dream in front of me. Achieving one dream led me to the next dream and the next dream and the next dream.

I always wanted to go to college. That wasn't a dream or an option, it was a mandatory necessity in every plan for success I had ever devised for myself. Morehouse wasn't my first choice for college, but it was the right choice. I had a full ride at Prairie View A&M, but I wanted to go to Harvard. I wanted the best because I wanted to set myself up for as many guarantees for success as possible. I don't remember ever receiving a response from Harvard, but my Mom, always supporting me in any and every way she can, encouraged me to apply to Morehouse. She knew I wanted the prestige, the WOW factor of an elite college or university, and she convinced me I could get that at a historically Black college or university (HBCU). My Mom always knew what was best for me, because once again she was right.

Most people go to college to find themselves, but that wasn't what I was there for. I knew who I was and what kind of man I wanted to be long before I stepped on that campus. The foundation of my character was formed in Missouri City, Texas. The foundation of my business was built on the campus of Morehouse College. To think I almost made the decision to stay home in Texas for college.

Reminder, I was accepted to Prairie View A&M (PV) with all tuition and fees paid, a full ride. My Dad drove me the fifty miles from Missouri City to Prairie View to attend new student orientation. While at new student orientation, I was told the scholarship awards I was awarded along with other financial aid I had secured would be more than enough to cover the full tuition. At this point, my Dad was fully sold on me attending PV because this totally relieved him of any financial responsibility for me going to college. But even with my Dad's approval and the finances for school fully secured, I still didn't feel right about it.

Once my Pops dropped me back off to my Mom's, I shared the news with her. My Mom, just as my Dad, was excited about the opportunity for me, but she could see I wasn't excited. During my time in high school, I had worked hard to earn the necessary grades and actively participated and excelled in extracurricular activities to make me an ideal candidate for acceptance to an Ivy League school. I had graduated from Westbury Christian School as one of the top ten students, not percent, but top ten actual people in my high school class. I wanted and believed I should do something a little more prestigious than staying at home for school. My Mom agreed and encouraged me to attend Morehouse.

The college experience I had pictured for myself included a campus of both men and women, so learning Morehouse College was an all-boys school almost deterred me from applying. However, I applied anyway and was accepted. Unfortunately, I wasn't offered a dime of scholarship money to cover the cost of tuition. The stress of not receiving a scholarship was made even heavier due to fact that the Morehouse tuition was double the cost of that at PV. So not only did I now have to pay tuition, I would have to pay double the amount I would have had to pay if I had gone to school in state.

Even with the cost of tuition hanging over my head and no clue to how it was going to be paid, I stayed focused on attending. I decided to go to Atlanta for a pre-summer program to get the experience anyway. During the summer, I made friends and got acclimated to the campus. At this point, I knew for sure Morehouse was where I wanted to go to college, and I was not willing to go anywhere else.

My mom was in full support of my decision to continue pursuing Morehouse, but everyone else in my family wasn't. Some of my family members actually begged my Mom not to take loans to pay tuition. These same family members also pleaded with me to stay at home and go to school for free. However, nothing is ever free.

I was determined, and I had a plan to succeed. I assured my parents and family members that everything was going to work out. I told everyone around me that I was going to do so well my first year that I would earn a full scholarship and continue to get full scholarships every year after that. As with most, if not all plans, mine didn't materialize as planned.

I did my part to ensure the steps I could control were executed as planned. Even though I did well and earned exceptional grades, I was only awarded a partial scholarship. Needless to say, the, "I told you so" and "you should have gone to Prairie View A&M" were once again vocalized by some of those closest to me. As much backlash and ridicule my Mom and I received from family and close friends about my choosing and her allowing me to go to Morehouse, we were both still determined to make it happen.

The reality that determination alone is not always enough hit both of us, and we were once again faced with the issue of not being able to afford my tuition. It almost hurts me to say that, at the time, I started feeling like some of my family members and friends that told me not to go were right. Some even seemed like they found satisfaction in knowing we were struggling.

I spent the first two weeks of freshman year at Morehouse moving into a dorm, going to classes, making new friends, and becoming more acclimated to the campus, just to one day see a letter on my door stating I had a balance owed to the school that if not paid I would have to move out. That day, my Mom and I spent hours in the Morehouse parking deck calling every bank and loan company trying to figure out how I would pay to continue to stay in school. After hours sitting in a hot car with no air conditioning, we decided to call my Uncle. This Uncle, my great Uncle, whom I had not spoken to in years, accepted my call. My uncle spoke to me for about thirty minutes, and at the end of the call, he decided to sign for a forty-seven thousand dollar loan that would cover my tuition for the first year. I promised him that not only would I pay him back one day, but I would also buy him a new car.

That loan made all the difference, and even though I never earned a full scholarship, I kept up my end of the bargain and followed through with my plan. I did well, made good grades, earned a partial scholarship, and a whole lot more after, but I also paid my uncle back years down the line. I tried to pay an extra twenty thousand dollars, but he wouldn't accept it.

My years at Morehouse College were pivotal. There were many impactful experiences over that short period that taught me major life lessons that will forever impact my life. Aside from the financial burdens over my tuition, another challenge was learning and developing new ways to connect with people. During my middle and high school years, playing basketball had been my catalyst to make friends and meet new people. However, I was not on the basketball team. This forced me to find new ways to connect with people and overall network. It forced me to grow.

Freshman year, I lived on the first floor, the ground floor of a residential building at Morehouse. I managed to build a crazy bond with guys I met on the first floor, and those guys became more than friends, they were my Morehouse family then, and they are part of my family now. Ironically, those same guys are not only still my friends, but a few of them I built my business with from the ground up. I met them on the bottom floor of a dorm at Morehouse College, developed some of the most instrumental relationships in my life, and together we all elevated on major level.

BT Lesson

DON'T ACCEPT OTHER'S FEARS

People will try to project their fears on you, but don't allow them to stop you. Safe isn't always secure. Prairie View offered a safety net, but Morehouse, while there was no net, provided an experience I could only gain from being at Morehouse.

I've come to realize just from my experience of paying to go to Morehouse there is always a price to pay. You've got to pay to play. Whether it's a monetary payment or it costs you time, energy, or some form of sacrifice, you always have to pay, at least for things worth having. Nothing is ever free. Most of the time, giving up your desire is the most expensive. It would have cost me more than money if I had listened to my family and friends encouraging me to go to PV for free rather than pull out loans and break the bank to go to Morehouse. It would have cost me much more than money if I had settled for free.

Not saying that my family and friends felt this way, but sometimes people will turn you away from the thing you set out to do. One, because they may be scared of what you will become once you achieve it, or two, they are afraid of the courage you have to pursue it.

Don't allow people to project their fears on you, which can also be a form of envy. People will try to project their fears on you because they're envious of your courage. Be leery of the, "Aww, you can't do that." It's not that you can't do it, they just may be upset at the fact that they can't. People may have been envious of me going to Morehouse. Who knows? Morehouse turned out to be the best decision of my life. Now there's a lot of people that see the outcome and now choose to support. I find it interesting.

It's never about you, and it's not always from a bad place. Or at least a consciously bad place.

It is important to be aware of people trying to attach themselves to you. As success comes, so will hype, and hype draws people in crowds. When hype and success come, it seems like everybody is your friend. Identifying who is really there for you or there for the success is important. Now I ask myself, "Would they be down to ride if they had to supply the vehicle, gas, and insurance as well as drive?" If there is even a hint of doubt, I regard it and them as what it is, just hype and hot air.

It's popular to hear people talk, rap, and post about moving in silence. The funny part is most people say this and turn right around and post and tell it all. Making moves is about more than the actual move. Before you can make a move, you have to first determine where the move is going to take you, then how you're going to execute the move and develop a plan of action and know a couple of plans of action to counter the move if it doesn't happen the way you originally envisioned it. Every move has to be intentional. It's important to know when to speak and when to listen. It's even more important to know who to talk to and to be aware of who is around when you're talking. This may mean keeping your thoughts and ideas to yourself even from your friends and family. Not because they will try to steal it necessarily, but sometimes people can get so excited they unintentionally reveal things that weren't ever supposed to be revealed. Because once you tell someone, just one person, it's no longer a secret. You can't be nonchalant and loose with information or plans that you set out to become successful or to accomplish something. If you plan to be a millionaire and have a plan or idea to get you there, you have a million dollar idea. Treat it as such. Discretion is key.

There is a quote that says "we're arrogant when we assume we'll have another chance to capitalize on an opportunity after taking our time for granted." In the past, I slowed down to allow others to catch up. That may be my biggest regret. You can't slow yourself down to make others happy. It doesn't work.

I never looked for handouts. In fact, I looked for ways to get a hand in.

Chapter 5

FIFTY OR FIFTY MILLION

I made fifty. This was my first wire transfer of fifty dollars, but it may as well have been fifty million because the same way that I made fifty dollars, someone else somewhere in the world made fifty million. The only difference is they had a lot more money to invest than I did. At the time, I was a struggling college student, and fifty dollars was a lot to me. Even now, there are people in other parts of the world who could take fifty dollars and feed an entire family. Think about homeless people in America. Just like those people don't take fifty dollars for granted, I didn't take that fifty dollars for granted then, and I still don't take it for granted now. Earning that initial fifty dollars by clicking a button on my phone without really knowing what I was doing let me know if it was possible for me to make fifty then it was just as possible for me to make fifty million the same way. Then I started to think beyond myself and think about how many other people could do the same exact thing. People that may possibly have had ten times as much knowledge as I did. Or better yet, ten times as much money as I did.

I spent the summer of 2017 in Cleveland, Ohio, working in an engineering plant as an intern. Not only was I going to spend the summer working and living in a new city, but this internship put me one step closer to being a full-time engineer. Most of all, I was going to be making twenty-five dollars an hour, which was considered good money, especially for someone my age. At least that's how I thought at the time.

Once I started working, my willingness to show up to work every day became slimmer and slimmer. I realized my motivation to be an engineer was not actually about being an engineer. I had subconsciously forced myself to pursue engineering because the most successful people in my family were engineers. So, I had seen engineering as my future and foundation to build my success upon at the time. But while interning, I realized engineering wasn't what I wanted but rather success, and I had accepted engineering as the vehicle to get me there.

I was conflicted because while still grateful for the opportunity, I wasn't excited. I hated the flatline day-to-day feeling of my internship. It was not at all exciting sitting in a cubicle, logging into a computer to check my e-mail with the hope of something interesting coming through to gain my interest and motivate me to continue. I detested the feeling of being on the clock, sneaking into work if I was a few minutes late. On top of this was the anxiety of the potential rejection of not being chosen to return as a full-time employee. Now I can't believe I even thought like that. Hate is a strong word, but in full honesty I hated it all.

As the checks from my internship progressed, I started to accumulate more money. As the money started to build in my bank account, I began to think more about how I could leverage this money to make more money. I started to focus on the potential ways I could take the money I had earned from my internship and leverage it to transition to a career I enjoyed. In short, I wanted to find something I really wanted to do that would produce the success that I wanted.

The experience of having a job wasn't all bad for me though. Working that internship taught me a lot of different things. One of the main lessons I learned was the importance of and how to manage my money. Most time, experience is the best teacher, and I had to experience both getting money and losing it, realizing I had spent it all.

My internship was the first time in my life I had made a significant amount of money. I was getting paid on a weekly basis. The more times I got paid, the more money I spent. I started spending way above my means. I was buying more clothes and eating out more. You could say I was living my best life, or so I thought. Well, my best life came to bust when I looked up after thirty or so days into my internship and realized I hadn't saved so much as a dime. It was then and still is crazy to me now that I had spent up my money because that whole entire time I was thinking, "Once this internship ends, so does my income." But the internship wasn't half-way over, and this is when I really focused not only on cutting back my spending to save my money, but also my need to figure out a way to keep this income coming in well beyond the internship.

As I have said before, I do not believe in luck or happenstance. I believe everything happens for a reason, and it happens when it is supposed to happen. And just as I believe, the timing was perfect when my older brother began reaching out to me about something he had been investing in. He started sending me screenshots to show me something he had invested in called BITCOIN. Of course, everyone knows what this is now, but back in 2017, nowhere near as many people knew what it was. He was making money day trading, and he told me he thought it was something I should probably look into.

Needless to say, all of this got my attention. I had been looking for something like this, and I inquired further. I was confident this was legitimate because I not only looked up to him, but I trusted Branden. He was a full-time engineer at the time, and not only did I respect what he said because of our relationship, but he was in the position I wanted to be in. My brother had achieved success via the traditional college education, corporate career, but now he had what I considered to be a better way and a way to achieve more. More than just a way to achieve more success, it was a way to do it on my own terms.

After I did my research, I decided to give it a try, and the first time I did it, I made money. Without any extensive knowledge or even really knowing what I was doing, I made fifty dollars. To be honest it was on accident. It still seemed crazy to me how simple it was and still is. The reality was affirmed when I withdrew the money from my investing account to add to my banking account. It was real.

I remember being at my job on my lunch break when I did the same thing my brother did. I sent a screenshot of my earnings to my college group text with my friends. Sending that text was almost second nature. I didn't really think about it. There were no intentions or agenda behind it. I just wanted to share the information and opportunity with them. I wanted to show them I had made money even though I didn't really know how or fully understand the ins and outs of trading. I wanted them to look into it because, at the time, a lot of my friends were also working internships in different cities, and they had the same mindset as me about sitting in a cubicle as well as similar goals for success, I wanted to put them on the same way my brother had put me on.

I would say, "to make a long story short," but this is a book, so I'll just tell it. Immediately after I sent that group text, one of my friends called me, and he didn't waste too much time asking questions before he said, "I'm with it. I want to make money. What do I need to do?"

At the time, I didn't know exactly what he needed to do. All I knew to do was share what I had done, and that is how I got him all set-up. I explained to him that I paid for an educational platform that basically helped me learn about the space of investing, and he immediately bought into it. Days later, I had a few other friends who decided to buy into it as well. I didn't know it until I received my first check that I was also getting paid residually as an affiliate business owner with the platform I was introducing my friends to. Not only was this my first time investing into different currencies, I was also getting a good taste of what it's like to really build a business.

I continued to gain results, and my gains started attracting more people, more people to buy into what I was doing. Things were getting more and more real for me as an entrepreneur.

I enjoy seeing others accomplish their goals almost as much as, if not more, than my own accomplishments. I enjoy it even more so when it is off the strength of me telling them about an opportunity, or they were inspired to take a leap of faith because of something I did or shared. So, after I verified the legitimacy of investing and trading, as well as put it to the test, I shared this information with my friends and college classmates because then, and now for that matter, all of us could use fifty dollars. Some eagerly accepted the invitation while others dismissively declined. It's funny now because I had more "No's" than "Yeses" but my belief in what I was doing didn't require more acceptance but rather required more rejection because ultimately it was the "No's" that kept me motivated. Back then and still now, I can get ten "No's" and one "Yes," and that one "Yes" will outweigh those ten "No's."

One rejection stood out more than others because it came from one of my closest college friends who said, "No," after I had fully explained with excitement and one thousand percent confidence that she would say yes and join me as the other people had. She told me that she would join once and if I could show her that I had made fifty thousand dollars. At the time, it was a little discouraging because I hadn't made anywhere close to that, but at the same time it was encouraging. It didn't matter if she was being sarcastic or not, her requiring me to make fifty thousand dollars before she would join actually helped me believe that it was possible.

Eventually, I made fifty thousand dollars, but by that time she didn't even come to mind. I had continued what I was doing. I started making more and more money, not only as an investor but also now as a business owner. Almost a year went by before I reached back out to her, and at this point, I had made more than fifty thousand dollars. Not only had I made more than fifty thousand dollars, this was now my main source of income. She still declined the invitation. She waited until I had made over a million dollars before she joined, but this time I didn't invite her. She invited herself.

Had she joined when she was initially invited, she would be much farther along. She set a standard for me that at the time she had not, nor did she have a plan, that I know of, to meet herself. She wanted me to have fifty thousand dollars when, at the time, I knew we would both be grateful for just fifty. She almost missed an opportunity because of her skepticism, doubt, fear, and her judgment of success. She not only declined the invitation, but waited so long that she had to be grateful the opportunity to invite herself was still on the table.

BT Lesson

SMALL WINS ADD UP TO BIG WINS

The lessons here are almost endless. The first is everything starts small, and small wins add up to big wins. Every one of my wins started off small. Every celebrity had a point in their life when no one knew them. Every great invention was once just an idea. Ultimately with this lesson, everyone's price is different. A lot of people miss out on creating something great because they only measure great things when they're small, when they're just a seed. Remember the tallest oak tree was once just a seed.

The next lesson is success is fluid and it has many levels. We all define success differently, and everyone achieves different levels of success at different times. Your success now can be different from your success ten years from now, and success is not just monetary. It's important to remember this. Every time you learn a lesson that you accept and apply, you achieve success.

Don't allow others to define your success because everybody has different definitions, dreams, and goals of success. What's success to you may not be it to the next person, and what's an accomplishment to the next person may not be one to you. One person may view success as making a million dollars, while you may have a goal of ten million and another person may view it as one hundred million. Then there are people who don't equate it to money at all. But guess what, every one of these are valid examples of success. If you get so caught up on a predetermined level, you could miss out on creating something that could create unimagined levels of accomplishments and profits for you as well as others. And that creation may be just what you need to get to a place you thought you couldn't go to or reach a level that you thought wasn't there. I understood with success making money is the easy part. The hard part is knowing the power in it and knowing what to do with it. Fortunately for me, not only did I make the money I understood the power in it as well. My first fifty dollars didn't seem like a big deal to a lot of people, but to me, it was the key to open gates of opportunity for myself as well as my peers. It's not the money, it's what the money can do.

My first fifty dollar wire transfer wasn't a big deal to a lot of people, but now reaching the level of success that I've reached from earning that initial fifty dollars has afforded me the ability to travel around the world and experience different cultures. There are parts of the world where fifty dollars may feed a person for a week, and in other parts, it may feed a family for a month. If I would have gotten caught up on the fact that fifty dollars wasn't a lot of money or that it wasn't life changing for me being a citizen in the United States, it would have kept me from continuing on a path that was not only life changing for me but also potentially positively impacting the life of someone else. That first fifty dollars helped me build a business worth over fifty million, because as easy as it was for me to make that first fifty dollars, it was easy for me to help others do the same. Now I'm helping tens of thousands of people around the world do the exact same thing. Help a little make a lot, or help a lot make a little. I chose to help a lot, because whether they made a lot or just a little, they made something and now had the opportunity to make and do more.

Do not judge people on where they are today. It's not wise to judge at all, but if you must impose an opinion, base it on where they're going and how they make decisions. When I first got started in business, I told so many people about what I was getting started and where I envisioned it was going to go. Some believed it, and a lot didn't. My classmate, my friend, had judged me on the fact that I was still working a job, didn't have a nice car, and I had no prior education in finance or the industry as a whole. She was judging me on where I was at that specific point in time. Now that I look back on it, I'm glad she didn't believe in my vision. When I spoke to her back then, I had only made my first fifty dollars, and that was enough for my vision to seem real. That was the difference between us. She needed to see fifty thousand to believe. Not fifty thousand dollars of her own, but someone else's. The most successful people don't cultivate a vision from success materialized or already in motion. They try to catch potential success at the slightest hint of the possibility and then cultivate a vision from that. Successful people are more stable than the stock market.

Don't be quick to discount or say no to people that don't have massive results right out or right now, especially when they thought about you early on in their vision for success. Stop trying to join what's hot, and start joining what's heating up. I could have gotten discouraged by her telling me no or challenging me to make fifty thousand dollars back then, but instead it motivated me. What she needed me to make back then overall, I make every few days. She believes me now.

You run fast for the win. You run faster for your life.

Chapter 6

JUST TWO OF US
AND THE BENZ

There is plenty to fear when you're Black and you hear the siren of a police car and see those lights flashing behind you signaling for you to pull over. To be a Black man in America is to know the dread of getting stopped by the police for no reason or explanation why, and simply complying or exercising your right to inquire about the reason for the stop could result in you ending up in jail or worse, dead. Even when the stop is legitimate and the cop is just doing their job, for Black people in America, we experience a level of anxiety that I don't think other races share. This time was no different. To this day, it still has been one of the most unanswered experiences of my life.

The measurement of success in America is something I think a lot of people have a hard time accepting. One of the status symbols and marks of substantiated success in America is the type of car you drive. Above degrees and clothes, pulling up in a certain type of car can automatically bring you levels of respect that other things that are obviously a lot more important cannot.

And I, still a college student at the time, had reached a new level on the ladder of success when I purchased my first Mercedes Benz. At twenty-one, I was the owner of one of the most quantified and accepted symbols of prosperity, a black Benz, LOL. This was an accomplishment for me, and the feeling of driving it off the lot was just different.

It's almost impossible to avoid small towns in Georgia when traveling. My friend and I were headed back to Atlanta from North Carolina, where we had moved to go to school for a dual degree program. We were passing through some small town in Georgia where we didn't look like the population, so I was trying to speed through. Even though all my stuff was legit, I still felt like I was doing something wrong being young, Black, and in a nice car when those red and blue lights started flashing behind me. Something inside me told me I wasn't just going to get a ticket and go home. I had a bad feeling, and as I sat with my hands on the steering wheel, I looked at my friend and I can only imagine what my face looked like, but I could tell he was thinking the same thing I was. "What are we doing wrong?"

He was looking at me wide-eyed but still being positive, repeating, "Bro we're good, you haven't done anything wrong."

But I could tell this was one of those times he was trying to be positive in a situation he was still unsure of himself. Unfortunately, I was right. I was arrested, but he wasn't. Once the officer told me to step out of the car, I knew I was going to jail. Part of me knew I didn't do anything wrong, but part of me was like, there has to be something they're going to find.

Before he even asked me for my driver's license and registration in the most country, in the middle of nowhere accent, he asked, "Whose car is this?" The "boy" was in the air even though he didn't say the word. I was waiting for him to end the question with "boy," but he never did. The blond-haired, blue-eyed cop cast that look that I was hoping I would never get. He had racist written all over his face. I could just see the hatred in his eyes. It's not a Caucasian specific thing, but more so a racist thing.

After I told him it was my car, he just stared at me before he told me he pulled me over for speeding, which is typically not a big deal. I followed all the protocols of keeping my hands where they could be seen, not making any sudden moves, and being polite as I handed over my license, registration, and proof of insurance as requested. Instead of the cop coming back with a ticket for me to sign, he told me to step out of the car. As I started stepping out of the car, he started to clench at his gun and brace himself as if he was about to pull it out on me and shoot, as if I were a threat. Still clenching his gun, he told me I was under arrest. As he cranked the handcuffs on my wrist, I assumed I had a warrant for something I wasn't aware of.

I thought I would get to the police station and make a call to my lawyer and leave, but that was not at all the case. I ended-up going to jail, and to this day I honestly fully don't know why. There was no interrogation or opportunity to explain that I was just passing through heading back to college. What I do know is I was locked up, in an orange jumpsuit confused as ever, with a bunch of other people who knew exactly why they were in there. They placed me in general population and told me I would have to stay for ten days. Not only was I confused as to why I was in jail, when they told me I had to stay ten days, I had made it up in my mind that they thought I was someone else.

Eventually, my fraternity brother who also happened to be a judge, got word of my situation and had me released immediately. Otherwise, I could be writing a totally different story right now.

I look back on that situation and realize cops really make no effort when it comes to arresting Black people to ensure they are arresting them for the right reason. Black automatically makes you "fit the description." Any sign that a Black person could potentially be doing something wrong is a crime within itself. It's even more of a crime when you're Black in a nice car, and don't let the car have temp tags like mine did. You're almost automatically going to jail. Like when I look back at it, young, Black, middle of the night, Benz, temp tags, random city...I should have known I was breaking the law, lol.

WE ALL GET LIFE

No one is exempt from what life brings and how the world is. Being successful won't necessarily exempt or protect you from the biases and prejudices of society. However, you can't let it discourage you from doing what you set out to do.

No matter how high you climb on society's success ladder, you are not exempt from the challenges of life. Never allow yourself to believe you are invincible because no one is untouchable, let alone invincible. At some point everyone, no matter how big your bank account or how elevated your status, gets tested. Don't allow those trials to break you.

Having nice things will bring attention, and all of it won't be positive. Everyone deserves to enjoy the fruits of their labor, so don't ever feel bad for earning and having nice things.

Don't accept boundaries, limitations, or ignorance from others. Don't allow others to contaminate or impose limits on your thought process. Don't accept stereotypes as your destiny. Don't think you don't deserve something, tangible or intangible, based off of things you have no control over like your skin color, where you come from, how old you are, etc. Success doesn't discriminate, so don't accept the imposition of discriminatory limitations.

This goes without saying, but I will say it because it's always worth saying. Time is always precious and never fleeting, so don't take it for granted.

Also, it's good to know it's not always what you know or who you know, its who knows you, and what for.

You either quit and put yourself right back in the position that made you start or you keep going and make the reason you started the reason people follow you forever.

Chapter 7

STAYING ABOVE WATER OR DROWNING

The first two years as an entrepreneur were not the easiest. When I first started establishing my business, it was hard. To any outsider watching, I'm sure it looked like I was drowning. On the other hand, some people may see a two-year struggle as an overnight success, but it was not. When you look at two years, it's ultimately not a lot of time based on the amount of success you gained. It's about how you spend those two years that make it long or short. If you spend the two years focused on the things that helped you reach your goals, then I think you can say the success came quick. But if you spend two years where nothing else matters and you move your goals to the top or second to whatever higher power you believe in, maybe sometimes above your family and friends, that can be considered a long time. Who's really willing to go two years straight mainly focusing on one thing and one thing only? Not too many people, but I was. Two years of doing the same thing over and over again and being so focused to the point where nothing else matters can be considered a lot longer.

I wasn't totally drowning as an entrepreneur, but I wasn't actually thriving either. I didn't start off making hundreds of thousands of dollars. I made a few dollars here and there, but in those first two years, I never made enough money to fully support myself. In full honesty, I would not have survived those first two years had I not been able to leverage financial support from outside sources. I applied to every scholarship. I applied for every grant and every loan. I didn't get all of them, but there were some that I was able to eat off of until I was able to support myself financially. But I wasn't going to learn how to swim in business if I kept dabbing my foot in the water. I had to jump all the way in. Before I could surf or even swim, I had to get in and learn how to hold my breath under.

While I was experiencing the trenches of entrepreneurship through trial and error, I also studied the industry as well as the people in it who had achieved the levels of success that aligned with my goals. In all honesty, study is an understatement. I stalked them to a certain extent. Not real stalking, but like modern-day stalking. I would spend hours at a time on their social media pages and reach out to them in the DMs to ask questions. Sometimes they didn't even respond, but I did everything in my power not just studying what they were doing, but studying what they did to get to where they were. Some of those people would not believe how much I watched them.

Even though those two years weren't easy, now that I know what I know, they were two of my best years in business because it was in those two years that I made the conscious decision that not only was I not going to drown, I was going to swim faster than I had ever swam before. I was going to get as close as humanly possible to walking on water in my business because I was going to learn to surf in it. Once I got the slightest hint of momentum, I made the decision I would keep it afloat for as long as possible until I could walk on water.

Things picked up my third year, and when they picked up, they picked all the way up. Ironically, just as the biggest waves come in the early morning and late evening, sunrise and sunset, my biggest wave came during what was known worldwide as a dark or sunset period.

2018 was my second year in the business and in all honesty, one of the more memorable and tougher periods. I had gotten a small taste of success and lost it for the first time. All of it. I realized you can't be fully content with being somewhere and having something until you lose what you have and gain it back. In 2018, I had lost the small taste of success that I'd had, but by the end of the year I had gotten it back, even more than before. Other people around me and in my industry weren't winning in 2018. 2018 was a tough year for the other entrepreneurial leaders in my business as well. Misery loves company, so it could have been easy for me to look at the fact that they were struggling and think it was okay for me to struggle as well. I never looked at what they were doing or what they had. I kept my focus on what I could do for myself and for the people following me.

Once I regained the success I'd had before, I told myself I wasn't going to ever lose it again. I valued it. I cherished it a whole lot more. Sometimes when you reach success the first time, that won't be enough to really build the confidence you need to be great. Oftentimes, people reach success and they question whether or not it was by accident or whether or not it was right place, right time. Honestly, most success happens by accident the first time. But that's why it's important to have the experience of losing it and then gaining it back on purpose.

Going into 2019, my life really started picking up. I feel like the third year was the momentum builder, and then things thing took off in my fourth year.

The coronavirus came in like a sunset in late 2019, and by early 2020, things were dark. Everyone around the world was ordered to go home and stay in their homes for an unknown period of time. As if being forced to stay inside wasn't bad enough, going outside could result in you losing your life. The fear of the virus and the unknown about it was the worst of it initially, but as it developed into a global pandemic, most businesses began to be affected, and within less than ninety days, a lot of businesses were in trouble. Before summer 2020, a significant amount of businesses had failed, but mine did the complete opposite.

I was running a full-fledged digital business that could survive a stay-at-home order because it was not built around or boxed into the traditional brick and mortar, cubicle community, face-to-face, water cooler interactive environment. People could join the business and learn how to trade and make money with their phones. As a result of not being able to go to work for someone else, more people began to look for ways to earn a living working for themselves. By me having an established business that allowed them to do just that, tens of thousands of people began joining my organization. Like a tsunami, my company and my income grew in quantum leaps. I say like a tsunami because before the COVID-19 economic impact shook up the world like an earthquake, a lot of people regarded my business as a bottom level or illegitimate organization, but like a tsunami, my business literally made it rain, leaving financial blessings behind in the wake of a pandemic that left a lot of businesses empty.

I had gotten what I asked for, what I had prayed for. I had reached the levels of success that I knew I would reach, but based on the way things moved the first two years, it had definitely happened a lot faster than I thought it would have happened. This is when I realized once you get what you ask and pray for, your faith level increases. I believe the manifestation of the vision brings with it a faith that inspires you to always want more because as my success grew, my faith became stronger, and I wanted to do more.

I set unrealistic goals early on where the numbers didn't really match up in the physical, but they made a lot of sense in the mental and spiritual. In full transparency, I set goals not knowing certain things would happen. I set goals not knowing we would be in a pandemic. I set the goal without knowing tens of thousands would join. I set the goal not knowing people would lose their business because of the pandemic. I set the goal without thinking about the in between. I set the goal knowing I would get there but not knowing exactly how. I set the goal not knowing a worldwide pandemic would push me there.

The momentum of my business growth was massive and fast. I went from being a well-known individual in my industry to being a very well-known individual nationally and around the world. The more success I gained, the more I started to experience this weird feeling, a sort of nervousness. At first it was subconscious, but as the business grew, the nervousness grew.

My confidence is one of my go-to's, so I don't make it a habit of giving energy to nervousness or fear. Rather than allow the uneasiness to keep growing, I took the time to determine what was causing this feeling. I knew I wasn't stressed about the success because it was the type of success I had visualized for myself pretty much my entire life. That's when I realized I wasn't nervous or afraid about being successful or about losing what I had acquired and accomplished. The nervousness was coming from the fear of not accomplishing more. The fear of becoming satisfied in complacency.

I believed then and still believe now that I am too young to plateau, so I dug deep to pinpoint the reasons for my achievement and why I had gone from what to most was a two-year struggle to rapid, almost lightning-speed success. This is when I realized the momentum had picked up because I never gave it the opportunity to die down. Even when things appeared to be at a standstill, I kept studying and learning more about the business and stayed committed in consistently pursuing my goals.

This was a turning point because after this, the better things got, the more I started looking for new things to do and new goals to achieve. I was already looking for the next opportunity, preparing to take the next step and strategizing a plan on how to successfully execute the next idea. Just like waves, the opportunities became greater, the steps got higher, and the ideas got bigger. If the right idea popped in my head, it was executed. I didn't (and still don't) sit around celebrating the accomplishments. I thought a lot more and a lot harder on the next level, and it paid off.

I reached the top of my company in 2020. When I hit this position, I was living in LA at the top of my building in the top of my industry. It was the penthouse of the most expensive building in LA. It was wild. I was literally spending the price of a car on rent every month, and not a hooptie. Old dreams became new realities.

Most of the people that know me knew this was something I had dreamed about, so they expected me to throw the biggest celebration they probably had ever seen. But I didn't. I honestly didn't really talk about it too much when it first happened. And in full transparency, because these are intimate details right, it's actually been like this for the last two or three years of my life as far as my accomplishments are concerned. I have never really celebrated or showed emotions at the level people probably would expect. In all actuality I've probably done the opposite of people's expectations.

I think I still do that to this day, in all areas of my life. Most people don't understand, and a lot of people mistake a lot of my ambition as humility. When in reality I guess you can say it is humility. I never bask or show a whole lot of emotions about good things happening to me because as soon as they happen, I accept that it happened with the highest level of gratitude and then determine what is the next thing I'm supposed to accomplish. If I had to connect that to a reason or rationalize it, as much as I hate to say it, I'm scared of reaching my peak this early in my life. So I think there is a subconscious fear that reminds me to stay humble and motivates me to be incredibly successful. When most people celebrate, I'm working to find and accomplish the next biggest reason or thing to celebrate. It's hard to stay still.

It is true that many times not taking time to celebrate has taken the fun away from doing what I do. But I've learned to live for the moment as opposed to living in the moment. This is what motivates me. Sacrificing fun and celebrations is definitely a form of sacrificing happiness. At the same time, I have found myself most happy when I am motivated and moving in that motivational space to accomplish the next big thing that is going to have an impact that is bigger than the last one. This type of happiness, while typically not recognized or acknowledged with a party or popping the cork of a champagne bottle is a happiness that extends beyond a single moment in time. This type of happiness, while more mild, is sustainable. It is this type of happiness that creates those big celebratory, firework type moments that are CRAZY but ultimately short lived. If I didn't have this type of motivation,

I wouldn't have a reason, and without reason, there would be no continuous happiness.

When I first hit two grand a month in my company, I knew I was going to, at the very least, hit six figures. It was just like the surfing principle. As the wave begins to lose momentum in preparation to die down, the surfer is already looking for the next wave so they can make their move to get in position to get on top of it and ride it out. That's what I did. I continued to make sure the momentum was not only still there but increasing. What I did to get to two grand a month, I did the same things times ten and kept adding something else until I reached higher and higher. I'm still focused, multiplying, planning, executing, and staying ready to catch the next big wave.

BT Lesson

DON'T HAVE TIME TO FAIL

You can learn a lot from the sport of surfing. I've learned a lot from surfing as it pertains to life, especially the life of business. Have you ever really thought about how a surfer floats on top of the water for long periods? It's an interesting concept, but I totally understand it because of what life has taught me. Surfers manage to stay above water because they respect the water and they never get content with the current or last wave they surfed. In order to stay afloat and above water, they manage to know and look for the next wave they're going to glide towards before the one they're currently surfing dies down.

This is applicable as it pertains to my business or anyone's business because most people waste time and energy focusing on being pulled back. This takes away from the time and energy that they could spend strategizing, developing, and planning how they're going to move forward. Too much time looking back or looking back for the wrong reasons can limit and potentially kill your momentum, and I honestly think that's how you fail. The moment you start looking at or being so afraid of the negatives, is the moment you start to miss out on discovering the positives. This is how and when you lose your balance, fall off the wave you were riding as well as your surfboard, and miss the opportunity to see and catch the next wave. This is how you wipe out.

Looking back too long and for the wrong reasons is a wipeout. Looking down is how you drown. When your focus is dedicated to what you don't have, you totally ignore what you do have. When you don't acknowledge or recognize the resources and tools you have in front of you, you never take advantage of them. You may not have an office with a computer, but you have a pen, a notebook, Wi-Fi and a phone. If you sit pouting about not having an office and a computer, you will fail to see the power in the things you do have that you could leverage to make enough money to get you an office with a computer. This is when and how you drown because you've talked yourself out of even trying. You've stopped yourself from getting started. Believe it or not, this seemingly small principle is the difference between someone who is successful for a year as opposed to someone who is successful forever.

You can never be content with what you've done because as time moves on, it's all in the past. No matter how big the accomplishment may have been to me, I couldn't show true emotion because I didn't have time to rest in emotions. I was too focused on the next, the next wave because in order to maintain the momentum, I needed to be prepared. I couldn't spend time standing up on my surfboard or high-fiving on the shore because if I had, I would have missed the opportunity to ride the next big wave.

Growing up, my Mom used to tell me, "Son, you take life very serious for someone your age," and in reality, I actually do agree with her. But I've grown to accept being this way because my serious mentality is what kept me focused and not falling into the trap of taking anything for granted. I understood highs and lows early, and when I applied it to surfing, it made it even more clear. This principle of understanding how waves rise and fall quickly, and timing the rise and drop can be your elevation or your termination, has in many ways saved me, my family, and even other people's family from detrimentally serious situations that could have had a bad impact on their lives.

One of the most derailing things people will tell you is "you've got your whole life ahead of you" … You don't. I don't believe the general concept of this statement to be true. I think you have "this" life ahead of you, or at least the time you are fortunate to be left on this earth. After all, life is but a moment with every moment to be taken advantage of. And even though you may have another moment, it still doesn't mean you have your whole life ahead of you to be able to do what it is you've set out to do. You can't have your whole life ahead of you until you get to a place of being whole, and only you know when you feel whole. Until you feel like you've done everything you've set out to do, everything you've seen yourself achieving in your dreams, and you have no regrets or desires to do or accomplish something else, you only have your life ahead of you. You should be more conscious of how you spend your time than how you spend your money. You should be spending the time you have right now, working, grinding, and staying motivated to get to the places you've envisioned, to stay riding at the top of the waves. It is at and in those moments, you can say you have your whole life ahead of you.

first you figure out
what you want.
Next you find a
vehicle to get you to
the things that you
want.
Then you drive it
every day to get to
whatever destination you
set in the very
beginning.

Chapter 8
TEACHING TO LEARN

We lost our house when I was in middle school. My Mom was and still is an entrepreneur. At the time, she owned a hair salon, and that had been her only source of income. She had had a challenging year with her salon, and she just couldn't afford to pay the mortgage. That situation prompted my Mom to look for other entrepreneurial opportunities to make money. This is how she started looking into other industries, network marketing being one of them. She even started doing presentations in our home before we had to move out.

One day, my Mom went to a network marketing presentation event at someone's house that really impressed her. She came home and told Branden and I about how she had gone to this million-dollar home owned by this young Black man. She told us about the textured walls, high-end furniture, movie theater, and Rolls Royce and Bentley in the driveway. At the time, she wasn't one hundred percent sure of the young man's network marketing position in the company, but she said to me, "It would be nice to see you like that one day."

I was twenty years old when I got involved in network marketing. After making my initial fifty dollar profit, I was hungry and made it a priority to learn as much about the business as possible. I continued to make money trading crypto and foreign currencies, but the bulk of my interest was building my business as a business owner, which was ideal for a college student like me. My first year earnings were less than ten thousand dollars, which was a lot less than I was making at my job; however, I knew and understood the possibility and the opportunity in my business. Sometimes when you first go into business, the first year or two you've got to be willing to take a pay cut. Sometimes you've got to understand it's the rubber band effect. If you put an object in a rubber band and don't pull it back, once you let go of the object it will drop straight to the floor. But if you put the object in the rubber band and pull it back, once you let go, it will propel forward.

It was 2017, my first year in business. I was a full-time college student, home from school for the holidays when I came across a social media announcement for a network marketing event being held in Houston. I didn't have a car of my own at the time, so I drove my Mom's car to the event. I didn't have any expectations as far as the venue was concerned, but I just wanted to learn and be around people I could potentially study and gain knowledge from. However, when I pulled up to the address on the flyer, I knew I needed to be there. The event was being held at a someone's actual crib, but this wasn't a regular crib. It was more like an MTV crib.

When I walked in there were, two presenters and less than one hundred people inside. Both of the presenters were young. One was Caucasian and the other one was Black. The Black one stood out to me because it's not too often that you run into young, engaging Black people in environments like this. It wasn't until he had been speaking a while that I realized he was actually the owner of the house.

As he was presenting, I pretty much took myself on a tour. I started looking around the house. I looked at things that most people probably wouldn't pay attention to. He had this rich wallpaper, and each room had different flooring. There were multiple luxury cars in the driveway and a few more in the garage. The furniture in the house was probably as expensive as the house itself. The house was amazing, but there was something about the house. It had a familiarity to it. This house, the house I was standing in, looked almost exactly the same as I had pictured the home my mother described to me almost ten years before. I was twenty years old at the time, but my Mom had told me about the house she had visited when I was in middle school.

I called and told my Mom I thought I was in the same house she had visited back when I was a young'in back in middle school, but she wasn't in agreement. She said the guy who owned the home she had gone to was in a totally different company than the company I and the guy I was watching present were in.

Still feeling like this was the house my Mom had described, I went back to watching the guy present, and he mentioned that he was in another company prior to joining the one he and I were in. I called my Mom again to tell her this because the previous company he was in was the one she said the young, Black man she had met almost ten years earlier was in. As my Mom and I talked about the event, I had a full-circle moment. The house I had just attended the event in was in fact the very house my Mom had attended the event in almost ten years earlier. More ironic than that, the young Black man she told Branden and I about was the same dude I had just listened to.

As if that were not enough, he was the owner of the house. Over the past ten years, he had been successful in quite a few network marketing companies.

I didn't have an opportunity to speak to him that day, but as I continued to attend network marketing events, I continued to be in the same room with him and eventually had the opportunity to speak with him. During our initial conversation, I told him I was going to be making six figures the next time I saw him. Just as I had said, the next time I saw him, I was making six figures. This led to him inviting me to speak at an event that he hosted.

He became my personal mentor helping me to go from earning six figures to earning eight. I studied him to a tee and began hosting similar events of my own. I put on an event for the very first time in 2019, which I named iMillennials. The event is basically geared to highlight and inspire the millennial generation to become massively successful as entrepreneurs. You could say I went back to the classroom to take others to school by sharing what I learned. The first time I hosted it, I was a little nervous but excited at the same time. The first time we did it, six hundred people were in attendance, which at the time made it a crazy, successful event. The second time, the hotel conference got a little bigger, and about three thousand people attended. Months after the second iMillennials event, right before I was about to drop the information for IM3 (the third one), COVID-19 hit and washed away all those plans. It wasn't until almost two years later, when COVID-19 died down, that I had the opportunity to host the third one, IM3. This time I decided to merge multiple entrepreneurial industries. I mixed education with entertainment. This made the conference feel like a festival event and conference all in one. We were definitely doing it different.

Another full circle moment, the same guy who invited me to his event, and my Mom told me she wanted me to live like, is the same person that I call to come to my events now.

BT Lesson

SIDE TO SIDE IN A CIRCLE

I often use "7" a lot. I do this to get people's attention. Seven is the number of completion. Completion of a cycle; however, it's important to clarify that when one cycle completes, that doesn't mean the end but rather means the beginning of a new cycle. I had a full-circle moment that began when I was in middle school and had its first seven when I entered network marketing. There have been several cycles of completion since my Mom came home from that initial event, and the cycles are continuing.

We go places before we get there. We must first go there mentally before we can get there physically. My Mom served as an intercessory in my cycle for my business. Actually, both my parents did with their initial involvement in network marketing and exposing me to it. My Mom going to the event at the very house I would end up at for the same type of event ten or so years prior was her going there in the physical so she could come back and help me develop the mental picture I needed to bring me there physically ten years later. Her description is what made it possible for me to create the mental picture in my head that helped me visualize specifically where I wanted to be.

What you visualize at some point will materialize in your reality, and it can appear on a much bigger scale than you probably could imagine. Be mindful of your thoughts and how you see yourself because what you see in the mental manifests in the physical. It is very important to manipulate our vision. If I continue to put things around me of where I want to be, pictures, visuals, whatever the case may be, I am manipulating my mind to only want to see those things. I am naturally building a new comfort zone in my physical site. So, when I'm faced back in my reality, I'm no longer comfortable, and subconsciously it forces me to do things that can only put me back in the position to see the things that my eyes really want to see. That's ultimately where I want to go. That's ultimately what's on the pictures and the visuals that I surround myself with.

Previously, I told you my ambition is often disguised as humility, but it's normal to have less of a reaction to things you've already experienced or seen. The same vision and picture my Mom painted for me as a middle school student has now become my reality. My home, to my cars, my accomplishments, and the other things that I've been able to acquire are all in sync with that vision. I am less reactive because I've seen this for myself long before I actually acquired it in the physical.

You can only teach what you know. This is why it's important to be open to learning.

You're a mentee to become a mentor.
You're a follower to become a leader.

You're watching to one day become someone being watched. You're in the audience to one day be the person on the stage. Ask yourself, "How long is it going to take before I turn on the switch to be on the other side to complete the circle?"

It's never really the kind of vehicle, it's more so the person behind the wheel driving.

Chapter 9

LIMELIGHT LIMITS

In 2020, I made more money than I had ever made in my life. However, as a result of the pandemic, I couldn't buy anything because all the stores were closed. None of the things I wanted to buy or would even usually buy were available for me to purchase. I felt like a lion too big for his cage.

What most people probably don't know or realize is that my line of work can sometimes impose restrictions, so being under the restrictions of the pandemic added another layer of additional limitations. During the lockdown, I wasn't the only one with restrictions. The entire world was restricted.

I remember being at my house and almost feeling like I was going crazy, but what stopped the crazy feelings was getting to a point of realizing none of that stuff really mattered in the first place. The moment I realized the whole world was restricted, that made me reflect. This is when I started to try to identify and ask myself, "What makes me different from everyone else?"

This is when I really became aware of the difference between being rich in money and being rich in life, rich in relationships, and rich in happiness.

So instead of focusing on not being able to buy stuff, I focused on the things that made life good. The things that I couldn't buy. The lockdown forced me to do things differently. I started waking up earlier and meditating. I got more in tune with God and prayed a lot more, which strengthened my spirituality. I started, eating better and working out, which not only helped me physically but also mentally. The relationships I had with the people closest to me got closer.

The limitations of the pandemic forced me to do these things. When I look back, the pandemic gave me a lot more than it took away.

I remember when I found out the Rolls Royce dealership had opened up. I had planned to buy my dream car on my twenty-fifth birthday. But the dealership was open, I had made more money than I'd ever made in my life, so I thought I may as well get it now. After I purchased it, I didn't feel any of the feelings I thought I would feel when I drove it off the lot.

I couldn't post it on social media. I couldn't show anyone. Driving alone, right after I bought it, I still felt some type of emptiness, and I never felt what I thought I would feel driving it off the lot. Now, trust me when I tell you it feels good driving my dream car, and every time I'm in it, my frequency is raised. But the best feeling about the Rolls Royce has been driving it with people close to me riding in there with me.

BT Lesson

LEVERAGE IN THE LIMITS

What led you to it won't keep you motivated to stay in it. Right now, it's popular to sing, "Where the money resides," and catchy to be "on your grind" to "secure the bag." Most people don't realize, "Where the money resides," is more than a residence. It is also a responsibility rooted in reason. There has to be a reason that is bigger than money. Your motivation has to be about more than houses, cars, jewelry, clothes, and vacations. Your why should be bigger than you; otherwise, you'll just have money, and without purpose, money is just paper.

Most of us dream of success that is validated and verified with material things or the opinions and likes of others. We have all seen the athletes and rappers with expensive cars, jewelry, and houses. The social media images are imprinted on our brains, and we strive to achieve the same things as the way we validate and verify our own success. The desire to drive the fancy cars, rock the designer labels and jewelry can motivate us to pursue the same type of success. But what happens when you get the money, cars, jewelry, houses, and clothes? What happens when it is no longer about the cars, jewelry, houses, and clothes? What happens when the material things are no longer the attraction? What keeps you going? More than that, what happens when the very things you dreamed of having are the very things that keep you from doing all the things you used to do?

Being in the limelight has its limits; at times it's more limiting than liberating. My business imposes standards about posting on social media that limit what I can share. I don't show what I have to motivate and inspire others. I don't leverage my material wealth or lifestyle. I am not always able to talk about the things I have accomplished or who and how I've helped.

Being in this so-called limelight or public eye means people are always watching me to see what I'm doing. I'm always under surveillance, but everyone isn't watching for inspiration. I can no longer move freely, the way I could when I didn't have the success. I move on higher alert because it comes with the territory.

Making money definitely changed my life for the better. It made a lot of things easier for me, but it also made some things hard. People will always have opinions, and sometimes those opinions are easy to ignore. But for me, the scrutiny became harsher and more disrespectful the more successful I became. Rather than allow it to break me, I chose to use it as inspiration because as long as there are no limitations on my brain, my mind is free, so I am free. I can and have developed new ways to inspire and motivate others. Some will see the success and the judgment will eventually go away, and some, no matter what, will find a justification to keep on judging and their doubting, judgment and harsh criticisms will never go away.

84

A million dollars or a million followers, it all comes with a level of scrutiny and some form of limits.

Me being required to find different symbols of success has made me better because in looking at different ways to motivate more people my age, it helped me to find other ways to keep myself motivated as well. It helped me to understand where my real success was, in my spirituality, in my health, in my family and friends.

They aren't going to respect what you do until it's not just you.

Chapter 10
KISSES &
CURSES

The same backs you clothe can be the very backs that turn on you. Ridicule and judgement do not dissipate as you elevate. In some cases, the higher you climb, the harsher the judgement and sharper the daggers. Even when respect is earned, there is no guarantee it will be given.

People have opinions about me that aren't always the best. Judgment is a harsh and cruel thing that I find myself subjected to daily. The opinions of critics can be wild and deadly like drive-by bullets.

It's crazy to me how people so easily cast away their judgments in acceptance for what is popular or socially normal. People easily accept what they've been told is good even when it's been proven to be something other than good.

Network marketing has been given a bad rap. Some people regard it as illegitimate, but it's just as legitimate as any other five-star business, most times a whole lot more. A few years ago, people spoke harshly and cast judgment and doubt on crypto currency and mobile pay. Now look at what crypto currency is doing and how people are using mobile pay aps all over the world.

Judgment and ridicule come from speculation that is based on fear of the unknown, ignorance, skepticism, and rejecting the new while resisting to change.

I had to learn to manage the kisses and the curses because, like the ultimate betrayal, some, if not most, curses come with kisses, too.

I was still in college when I started the business. As I began to learn about crypto currency and trading, I became excited about the opportunity it provided, so I shared the information with other college students. In the beginning, more people were more interested in talking down on the opportunity than listening to me. A lot of the people that initially didn't believe in it were people I was cool with. They made memes about me and even cancelled my events once they found out what I was coming to promote.

It's said, "What doesn't kill you, makes you stronger," and that's true because industry ridicule transcends to winners in the industry. Even though the meme was made to mock me, it was actually free advertisement.

Even though I wasn't allowed to host the event as planned on that campus, I found other venues and hosted events that got bigger and bigger. I am actually in the process of planning an event at a stadium as I write this.

As much as I have tried to separate my personal and business life, they intersect. Before large amounts of attention and success, I met and networked with a lot of different people. The moment I met one, I would meet another. But when I became successful and started getting crazy amounts of attention, I came to realize the difficulty in meeting people who were genuine and had no regard for what I had or what I could do for them. It wouldn't happen too often that I would meet a female that didn't care that I made millions and had what I have.

I have met a lot of attractive females over the last four to five years I've been in business, but there was one that stuck out to me. Even though we were from different parts of the world, she demonstrated a lot of the same morals and character traits that I possess. She was one of the more genuine people I had met since I started becoming successful. Unlike all the other females I had met along the way, she never seemed to care about what I had, who I was in public, and more specifically, what I was doing business wise. She didn't ask me to pay for anything or expect me to buy her anything. In fact, she didn't want me to buy her anything, and I thought that made her even more attractive. To me, she displayed signs of independence and ambition that a lot of the other women I'd met didn't. Even though I could financially probably buy her anything she wanted, it was a breath of fresh air knowing she at the very least wanted to be able to take care of herself.

We met up a few times and started getting to know each other more and more. She was learning about me, and I was learning about her. We seemed to vibe and we started getting more and more comfortable with each other. As far as I was concerned, things were going well.

Initially it was refreshing that she had not asked about my business or financial status. However, as time went on, it seemed weird that she didn't even acknowledge any of it. I wear expensive jewelry, which she never acknowledged. She'd ridden in all these expensive cars, but she never said a word. Even though it's somewhat obvious what I do via social media, she never actually asked me.

We were out together one night when she asked me a question that took me completely left field.

"How long have you been scamming?"

I literally just looked at her, frozen. I wasn't upset but more so in shock and in my defense, I laughed in her face before I asked her, "What did you say?"

She boldly reiterated the same question, asking, "You know, how long have you been doing the investing thingy?"

As insulted as I could have, and probably should have been, I found it funny. I literally just laughed in her face. Not in a condescending way or even irritated way. I genuinely laughed because at this point, the judgements towards me and my business are hilarious.

We're still cool because at that point I realized she was still cool people, but definitely not someone I would take seriously or be in a relationship with.

Both my parents were, and still are, motivated and hardworking individuals. I watched them have several different businesses and have several different jobs throughout my childhood. One of the industries they kept returning to was network marketing. I would watch them host meetings, sell different products, and try different things. Now that I'm older, I realize it was the same industry, they were just going to different companies, changing products, so they never had massive success. At twenty, I was re-exposed to networking marketing, and I had a chance to try it myself. This time it seemed a lot different than what I was exposed to as a child. It seemed a lot fresher, a lot newer, and a lot more innovative.

I also realized it was a good opportunity for me to change the game that was already being played. As I started building and launching a network marketing business for the first time, I made the decision that I didn't want to do things the traditional way. I realized I didn't want to follow a script, but I didn't want to reinvent the wheel either. I just wanted to make it better. In doing this, a lot of people looked down upon it in the industry. But over time, they started to appreciate it because it worked. Even though this was my first time ever really being in the industry I achieved levels of success that people who have spent decades in the industry haven't. And as great as this was for my bank account, I still received more ridicule than I could have ever imagined.

I'm usually clumped in the same category as music artists, entertainers, and athletes as far as lifestyle and image, but the impact is very different. When you're a professional athlete, you get paid a lot of money, but the people that are inspired and support and want to be like you one day don't get paid anything. When you're a big music artist or entertainer, your fans increase your revenue, but the fans who watch and listen to you don't get paid anything. In the industry of network marketing, I've had million dollar months, but in the midst of the money I made, I've helped tens of thousands of people make money as well. Or better yet, I've had million dollar months, but in the industry of network marketing, that was just a by-product of me helping tens of thousands of people make money as well. It's funny that you know the industry of network marketing receives the least amount of support and respect but pays the most to all the people that support it. Whereas the NBA, NFL, major record labels, etc. keep the money they make for themselves. We support things and people and get paid nothing for it, but those that support network marketing businesses not only have changed their lives, but are changing the lives of other people they expose their business to.

BT Lesson

RESPECT TRANSCENDS RIDICULE

They aren't going to respect what you do until it's not just you. Not just doing it, but winning in it. You may not ever get love from hate, but when you stay down until everybody is doing well, you'll at least have respect. I'm not expecting the whole world to love everything we do, but just respect it. Three people, three million people, whatever the number is, it's not just one…that was never the plan. Being the only one is trash and overrated anyway. The people that were down in the beginning are the people that are up now. However, not everybody will stick around through the downs or even be willing to be there in the first place. The bottom isn't as crowded as people think because most people aren't willing to start there.

Unfortunately, when you're young and African American and you make a lot of money, you're living in a nice home or building, and have really nice things most people will question what you do if you're not an athlete, rapper, or entertainer.

Their judgment is not our cross to carry. Instead of allowing it to weigh you down, let it motivate you. It's not your responsibility to make them understand. It is your responsibility to believe in and respect yourself to continue to pursue your goals.

No matter where you are or what level you're at, somebody or people will always have something to say, especially in entrepreneurship. You make a few thousand a month as an entrepreneur, someone will say they make more at their job. You make tens of thousands of dollars a month, somebody may say you're scamming people or you're cheating people. You make millions of dollars, somebody will say you're not making smart investments. You start buying real estate, someone will say you're just renting. You Uber everywhere, somebody will say you don't have a car. You buy a car, somebody will say you leased it. You walk around in a nice outfit, somebody will say you don't have any jewelry. You buy some nice jewelry, somebody will say it's fake. You spend thirty thousand dollars on a watch, somebody will say you should have given it to your family. You give fifty thousand dollars to your family, somebody will say you should have given it to the community. You give a hundred thousand dollars back to the community, somebody will say you should have given a million. No matter what you do or how you do it, somebody will always have something to say. Don't allow what other people think you should do with your money to influence what you actually do because no matter what you actually do, they will always have something to say about what you should have done. And more often than not, those same people haven't experienced your success, so how can they know what to do with something they've never had! Listen to people in positions you want to be in.

More money less problems, more solutions.

Chapter 11
OWN THE
MONEY

I've hired people to work for me, and the relationships started off well. However, as my success grew, they expected theirs to grow too, and it did. The sad part is it seemed theirs didn't grow as much as they wanted it to. Instead of looking at ways to better market their products and services, they looked to me. As my price went up, so did theirs. Their price didn't always increase for everybody, but it did increase for me. Sometimes by a lot. I had helped them expand their business by promoting them to my friends, family and social media followers. However, they forgot that I'd helped them, and instead tried to charge me more because I had more. I don't appreciate people who forgot who helped them.

After you graduate from high school or college, most of your new relationships are made from contacts you meet in your professional interactions. It's not always easy for me because I have to watch every new person I meet. Being guarded in this way is not a selfish thing; I'm not just protecting myself, but I'm protecting others around me, the people I'm responsible for.

From the smallest favor to the biggest services, anyone who has offered to put a hand out to help me, I've learned to question it. I have to watch and be careful because I realize how easy it is to help someone when you know helping them a little can ultimately put you in the position to have them help you a lot. It's not always easy doing business with people at this point in my life. It's forced me to have a "no new friends" approach, more than ever.

At this point in my life, I wouldn't consider myself long money. Even though I have earned a substantial amount, I still consider myself new money. My life has changed substantially over the last four years, especially in business. My first year in business, I made less than ten thousand dollars. Year two, I made a little less than eighty thousand dollars. Year three, I made a little less than two million dollars, by year four, I was inching close to a ten-million dollar income. In addition to having much more money, the amount of people around me, both up close and personal as well as on social media and worldwide, grew. Year one I had less than a hundred global supporters. However, the number has grown tremendously. In my second year, I had reached close to a thousand. At the start of year four, that number had increased to seventy thousand in over ten countries.

For most people, that can seem overwhelming, and quite honestly sometimes it can be. Starting a business at twenty years old and now only being twenty-five, I feel like I've had to grow up in a short span of time. The last two years have felt like ten, and the last four have felt like forty.

BT Lesson

CHARACTER IS CURRENCY

The other week, my pastor asked the question, "How high can He lift you without losing you?" That question stuck with me. To the outsider looking in, and even those up close and personal, I'm on top of the world. But being on top of the world is not a place where God elevates you to sit and rest. To whom much is given, much shall be required is Biblical and true. I'm not here to flex, ball out, and spend money. No, that's not my purpose. I'm here because I have work to do.

I've learned after you make a lot of money, it's easier for money to leave your bank account without you knowing it. At some point in life, most people know when a single dollar leaves their bank account. As you make more money though, there could be instances when you may not even realize if a hundred or even ten thousand dollars leaves your account. There may even be some people in the world in a position to not notice or miss a million.

I'll admit that since I've become more financially stable, I don't notice every single dollar. Unfortunately, I have come across people who have attempted to take advantage of the amount of attention I pay to that at this point. I'm not happy to say I've experienced people trying to steal from me both directly and indirectly.

I know the average person my age doesn't have to deal with a lot of the pressures and the responsibilities I deal with. I guess the money and the lifestyle I live have been the requirement for me to make these sacrifices and accept the responsibility. It still can be a lot of weight on my shoulders. The weight isn't so much from the responsibility but more so the distractions. The distraction of not being able to trust people, having to be on high alert.

At this point in my life, I'm not distracted by money, cars, parties, and women. I find myself more so distracted and influenced by the people I surround myself with.

My environment has changed regularly and rapidly over the last four years. One environmental change can create a level of stress. A constant and rapidly changing environment can be overwhelming and uncomfortable.

I've been taught getting out of my comfort zone can help me grow. There have been several instances in my life where I had to decipher whether I needed to get out of my comfort zone or stay true to myself. I think when someone makes a lot of money, that comes up a lot, at least that has been my experience. I've learned that before you get out of your comfort zone you have to know when getting out of your comfort zone will help you or hurt you. Will getting out of your comfort zone have a negative outcome or positive outcome? Will getting out of your comfort zone take you out of your character?

This is one of the reasons I believe it's important to surround yourself around successful people and surround yourself around people who know something that you don't. But you have to be very careful that you don't sacrifice the relationship with the people who don't need you for anything, don't care about what you have, or who you can really trust.

I know you can go fast by yourself, but I also know you can go much farther with a team. Building a team that can work with you and work independently for themselves is a lot easier than building a team to work for you. I have met and hired people to support my business or secured the services of their businesses, and in a lot of these situations there were problems because their intentions were not the best or they were just lazy. Now that I know what I know, that really isn't about the money. That's about those people.

I've often heard people say, "Money is the root of all evil," but money in itself is neither good or evil. It is simply money, something we use to buy the things we want and need. Money isn't a seed that can plant itself, so where it takes root is solely due to the way and motive for which it is used. The power of money comes from us, from people. But people become slaves to money, measuring their own worth, capabilities, and purpose and sacrificing impact, integrity, and character. Character has no currency. Its value is immeasurable, and once compromised, its depreciation can be deadly. Compromised character can lead to death of relationships, business deals, etc. Too many people compromise character for a few bucks.

Look at the amount of our lives that we're expected to dedicate to making money. Literally a third of every day, eight hours, in exchange for money. A price tag on something that can never be bought, our time.

Money is a necessity, but I make the money, it doesn't make me.

People say, "more money, more problems," but I don't see that as truth. There will always be challenges because that's a part of life. Challenges are simply growth processes that require the most sweat. I say more money, more solutions. The more money I have, the more I can help others. The more access I have to money, the more capable I am to create more solutions and have a positive impact that is beneficial to others. It's up to me to dedicate the money to address problems that are outside of me.

There is an expectation that your bank account should define your character. Now that I have money, people expect me to be rude and arrogant. People expect me to buy this, do that.

I'd be a liar and a hypocrite if I didn't admit there are benefits to being wealthy. However, the benefits are not because of the money, but rather our beliefs and attitudes about money. I own the money; the money doesn't own me. And money makes a difference, it doesn't make us different.

The road to success is like a drug. I'm a proud addict.

Chapter 12

MY WHY AT 25

I'm twenty-five now. You don't have to be old to be wise, and being old doesn't guarantee you will develop wisdom. I mean, just think how many times you have encountered someone that you would regard as being an old fool. Many people avoid wisdom because they choose to stay within the limitations of the people, places, and spaces that they regard as being safe. So unfortunately, they miss out on a huge portion of their potential. That's when you end up drunk and dizzy with the regret of the "what ifs". There is a bliss in ignorance that I don't ever recall having the luxury to enjoy, and I'm not sad about it. Matter of fact, I'm glad about it. Yes, I carry the weight of wisdom, which is never light. Ironically, this is poetic because it's this acceptance of the responsibility and reverence for wisdom that has allowed me to take off. It was in wisdom that I learned that the reason for my success was bigger than me.

I always have, and I will continue to, move at my own pace. I don't allow other people's expectations to influence how I move. People think seventy thousand thoughts a day, and over half of them could be about someone else. I've learned to stay true to myself and grind. If I'm one of someone of else's thoughts, I want me being true to myself and my grind to be the why.

My reason now is not necessarily about the money. It's more so, seeing. I get the biggest thrill seeing people just like me, like how I was two years ago, and actually being able to watch them elevate. It's more so the impact now.

I asked to be in a better financial situation, once I made the money, once I got to that point of financial success, then it became about the impact. I wanted to have a positive impact on other people's lives.

Not only do we value the importance of our peers understanding investing, but we are committed to the exposure, empowerment, and investment within our peers as well.

I've been in tears watching my friends make millions of dollars. It's exciting. It's life changing.

"For many are called, but few are chosen." Matthew 22:14 KJV. This track of success chose me, and I am grateful to be one of the chosen. I'm still learning, still growing, still grinding and still earning. I am hopeful that each day will continue to bring reasons that are more valuable than money, bigger than me, and stand the test of time.

And no, this isn't last quarter talk. We treat every quarter like the fourth. It's still just the very beginning…

106

LEARNING IS LIVING

The experiences will continue, the lessons will keep coming, and I am determined to keep learning because as long as I am learning and in pursuit of what I want, I am living.

Afterword

People often ask me what I'm working on or what's next. I've learned you can't let them know what's next every single time. Some things have a bigger effect when it just comes out of nowhere, like this book. The element of surprise hits different every single time! ...and be careful who you share your plans with. Those that genuinely love you will be excited for the drop. Those that aren't will try to find ways to sabotage or beat you to it. This is just food for thought, and I'm still learning every day! Pay attention to the signs and act accordingly. Stay ahead of the game forever. God is the greatest!

Acknowledgements

Before I close out this book, I want to thank God, and I want to thank God for using me as a vessel. I never want to take full credit for anything I've ever done or anything I've ever accomplished because I never would have been able to do it without God or the people that have come before me. I find it easy to stay humble because everything that I've accomplished would not have been accomplished without the blessings from God and also the people He's placed in my life who've come before me. God has blessed me with the cash, so it's only right that I give Him the credit.

Huge, huge thank you to my mentors, role models, and people that have played that big brother role in my life throughout this journey as well as my actual big brother, Branden. They've made this journey a lot shorter than it had to be. I've been able to learn from not only the good things that they've done, but I've also been able to learn from the mistakes they've made as well. They've given me that perfect advice even being imperfect people.

Another huge thank you to my support system, my closest friends, the people I call brothers. It's a breath of fresh air knowing I've got like-minded individuals around me that not only want to be successful, they want to be successful with me, together as a collective. That makes the journey so much worth fighting through.

Huge shout-out to the people that have come into my life even after I gained success but still had positive intentions and still had genuine spirits and didn't want me for anything materialistic or monetary.

Huge shout-out to my Dad, probably the most competitive person I know. Huge shout-out to him keeping me motivated and inspired to go out and be a great, not only leader but a great man and individual.

Lastly, huge thank you to my Mom. I honestly don't even want to say too much because I don't think there are enough words that could describe my gratitude for her. I'll just end off by saying, thank you Mom. You're my hero.

About the Author

BRYCE THOMPSON is a serial entrepreneur, business builder, event planner, investor, philanthropist, business mentor, multi-millionaire, author and publisher.

At 23 years old, Thompson became the youngest, highest paid networker not only in his company, but in the world, ever. Now at 25, Thompson is a recognized leader in the global Crypto / Investment community.

Early in his entrepreneurial career his strong desire to teach and lead others to pursue their visions of personal success prompted Bryce to leverage his YouTube channel to share his experiences, lessons and success. "A day in the life of Bryce" did more than inspire a generation of young adults, it aided in building Thompson's brand.

His commitment to having a positive impact and passion for

education and bringing people together inspired the annual iMillennials edutainment conference and festival event (currently in the rebranding phase with a new name for the upcoming fourth event) and the IAMS Foundation which provides scholarships to students attending Historically Black Colleges and Universities (HBCU).

Thompson remains deeply rooted in the hope that his insights and influence will inspire others to "move far, not fast," when seeking success as an Independent Business Owner.

.

Printed in Great Britain
by Amazon